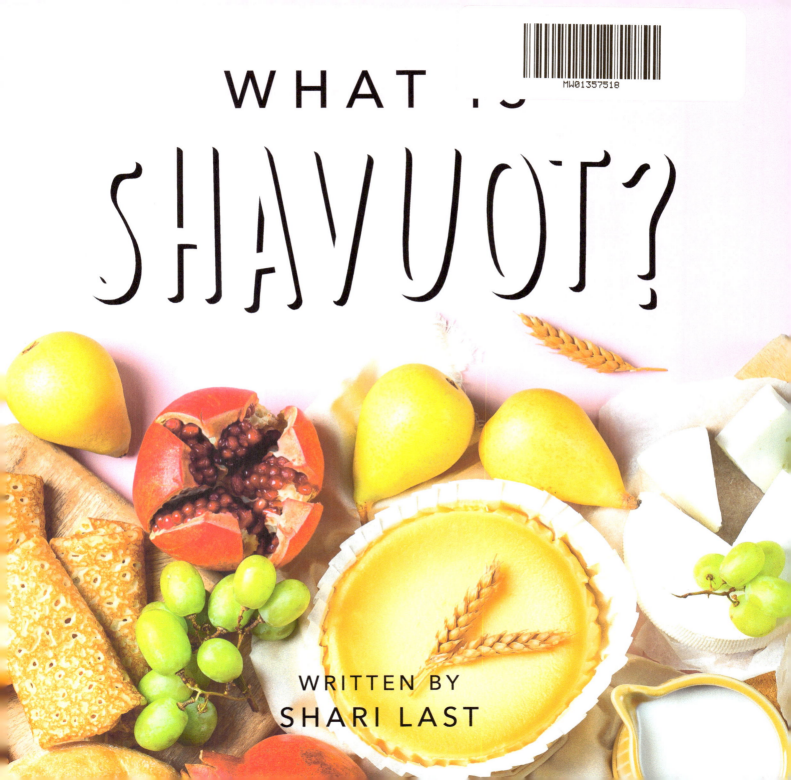

WHAT IS SHAVUOT?

WRITTEN BY
SHARI LAST

THE CELEBRATION OF A NATION

Cheesecake and flowers – that sounds like a pretty good holiday to me! Throw in a family meal, a trip to synagogue, and a bit of ice cream and you've just described Shavuot.

Shavuot celebrates the moment when the Jewish people became a nation. This happened when they received the Torah from their God and promised to live according to its laws.

THE TORAH
The Torah is the holy book of the Jewish people, and the guidebook to their way of life. It contains the history of the Jewish people and the laws they live by. Learn more about the Torah later on in the book!

A Harvest Celebration, Too!

Shavuot is also the festival of the wheat harvest, when farmers in the land of Israel would bring the first produce of the season to the Jewish Temple in Jerusalem.

Are You Ready To Learn All About Shavuot?

WHEN IS SHAVUOT?

Shavuot is celebrated on the 6th day of the Hebrew month of Sivan.

The Hebrew calendar is lunar, so Jewish festivals don't fall on the same day of the "regular" calendar each year. Shavuot usually falls in early summer, normally during the month of June.

DID YOU KNOW?
Around the world, Shavuot is celebrated for two days. In Israel, however, it is celebrated for just one day.

WHAT DOES SHAVUOT MEAN?
Shavuot means "weeks" in Hebrew. This is because it there are exactly seven weeks between Passover and Shavuot.

PRONOUNCING SHAVUOT

Shavuot is pronounced like this:
shuh-voo-ot.

Here's how it's written in Hebrew:

שבועות

SHAVUOT GREETINGS

If you have any Jewish friends and you want to wish them a happy Shavuot, here are a couple of ways to say it:

"HAPPY SHAVUOT!"

or

"CHAG SAMEACH!"

Pronunciation: *Chugg Sum-ay-ukh*
(This means "Happy Holiday" in Hebrew)

Note: the "ch" in "Chag" and "Sameach" is a sound you make at the back of your throat. Or you can just use an "h" sound.

THE STORY OF SHAVUOT

The story of Shavuot took place more than 3,300 years ago. The Jewish people had just escaped from Egypt where they had been slaves for many, many years. They were travelling through the desert...

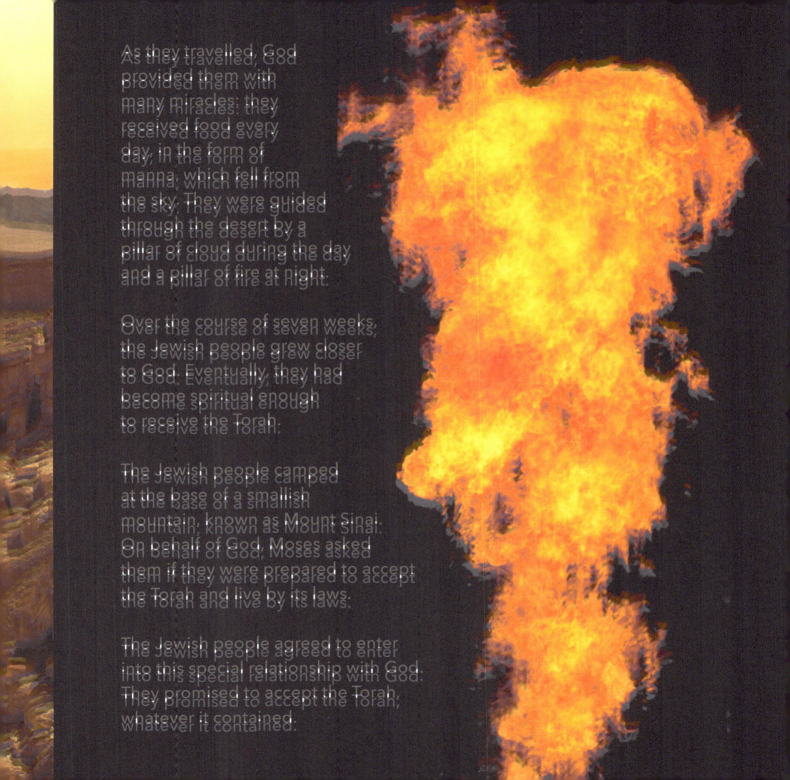

As they travelled, God provided them with many miracles: they received food every day, in the form of manna, which fell from the sky. They were guided through the desert by a pillar of cloud during the day and a pillar of fire at night.

Over the course of seven weeks, the Jewish people grew closer to God. Eventually, they had become spiritual enough to receive the Torah.

The Jewish people camped at the base of a smallish mountain, known as Mount Sinai. On behalf of God, Moses asked them if they were prepared to accept the Torah and live by its laws.

The Jewish people agreed to enter into this special relationship with God. They promised to accept the Torah, whatever it contained.

Over the next three days, the people prepared themselves to receive the Torah. Mount Sinai bloomed with beautiful flowers, even though it was in the middle of the desert.

After three days, the Jewish people stood at the base of the mountain, which was now shrouded in smoke. Lightning and thunder broke over the mountain and the sound of the shofar (a trumpet made from a ram's horn) could be heard.

Suddenly, everything went silent. Then out spoke the booming voice of God, reciting the Ten Commandments. The people were frightened by God's voice, but Moses told them not to be scared. Moses went to the top of the mountain, where he remained for 40 days and nights, writing down the entire Torah as instructed by God. When Moses came back down the mountain, he held the two tablets containing the Ten Commandments. From that moment on, the Jewish people had a special bond with God, and they kept the Torah laws.

WHAT IS THE TORAH?

The Torah is the first (and most famous) part of the Jewish bible. It contains the history of the Jewish people up until the death of Moses, and the 613 laws of Judaism. The laws of the Torah affect many parts of day-to-day Jewish life.

Torah Scroll

KASHRUT

Keeping kosher means eating, drinking and preparing food according to the Torah. There are many complex dietary laws, but here are some of the major ones:

- Only kosher animals can be eaten.
- Kosher animals must be slaughtered in a specific way.
- Meat and dairy foods cannot be mixed.
- Separate utensils and cooking equipment must be used for meat and dairy.

SHABBAT

The Torah instructs Jewish people to rest from work on the seventh day. So, on Saturdays, many Jewish people keep Shabbat – a day of rest. On Shabbat, we cannot cook, write, drive, watch TV, use electronic devices, or go shopping. Instead, we spend time with family and friends, enjoy sociable meals, and go to synagogue.

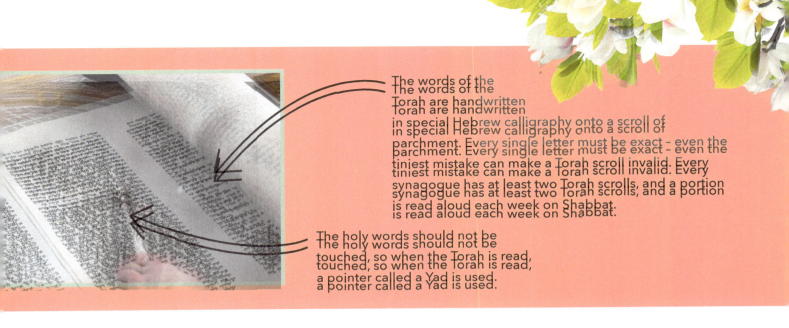

The words of the Torah are handwritten in special Hebrew calligraphy onto a scroll of parchment. Every single letter must be exact – even the tiniest mistake can make a Torah scroll invalid. Every synagogue has at least two Torah scrolls, and a portion is read aloud each week on Shabbat.

The holy words should not be touched, so when the Torah is read, a pointer called a Yad is used.

THE TEN COMMANDMENTS

These are the ten laws that the Jewish religion is based on. They form the basis of Judaism. Moses carried two stone tablets carved with the Ten Commandments when he came down from Mount Sinai.

1: I am the Lord your God
2: You shall have no other gods
3: You shall not say God's name in vain
4: Observe the Shabbat day
5: Honour your parents
6: You shall not murder
7: You shall not have improper relationships
8: You shall not steal
9: You shall not lie
10: You shall not be jealous

THE COUNTDOWN

Do you remember how many weeks there are between Passover and Shavuot?

That's right, seven. Which means there are 49 days between the two festivals. Many Jewish people count those days, one by one, all the way from Passover until Shavuot!

But why?

A SEVEN-WEEK JOURNEY

Passover celebrates the escape of the Jewish slaves from ancient Egypt. Think about it: the slaves left Egypt and walked through the desert. They were scared. They were tired. They knew nothing about life apart from awful slavery.

As they walked, they saw God's miracles all around them: how He sent them food and showed them the way. Day by day, the Jewish people grew less afraid. They became more spiritual, closer to God. Eventually, after 49 days, they were holy enough. They were ready to receive the Torah and follow its laws.

So that's why some Jewish people count the 49 days between Passover and Shavuot. For the slaves, each day was a day closer to receiving the Torah. Each day was one of the final steps on their long, long journey.

COUNTING THE OMER

These 49 days are called the Omer. To count the Omer, there is a short blessing to say each night, followed by the sentence: "Today is day [insert number] of the Omer."

BUT … If you want to say the blessing each night, you can't miss any days out! If you miss a day, you are out! Believe me, it is very tricky to make it all the way to the end of the Omer. I try every year, but I've only made it all the way through three or four times!

CELEBRATING SHAVUOT

Shavuot, like many other Jewish festivals, is a "work"-free day. This means many Jews do not go to school or work, drive, cook, spend money or use electronic devices. Instead, Shavuot is about spending time with family and friends, going to synagogue and enjoying big festive meals. Here are some of the Shavuot traditions that make the day extra special:

FLOWER DECORATIONS

Because Mount Sinai bloomed with the most beautiful flowers, it's a custom to decorate Jewish homes and synagogues with flowers and greenery.

DAIRY FOODS

When the Jewish people received the Torah, they learned the laws about food, drink and eating. These laws are very complicated, so the people decided to eat only dairy until they understood it all properly. So, on Shavuot, it's traditional to eat dairy-only meals.

ALL-NIGHT LEARNING

There's a legend that the Jewish people overslept on the morning they were due to receive the Torah! That's why some people stay up the whole first night of Shavuot, learning Jewish texts. This is known as Tikkun Leil.

TRADITIONAL FOODS

On Shavuot, it's customary to eat dairy foods. This is quite different to most of the other Jewish festivals, where the big family meals often include various meat dishes. One bonus of having a dairy meal means that Jewish families can enjoy ice cream for dessert!

KEEPING KOSHER
The rules of kashrut include not mixing meat and dairy, but there is another rule to wait three hours after eating meat before you can eat dairy again. (In some cultures, the wait is just one hour, while in others, it's six!)

CHEESECAKE
While many dairy dishes make an appearance on Shavuot, cheesecake is probably the most popular! Everyone looks forward to delicious cheesecake desserts. (And maybe even for breakfast too!) If you're getting hungry, there's an easy cheesecake recipe near the back of the book.

CHEESE SAMBUSAKS
Indian Jews eat savoury cheese sambusaks on Shavuot. The recipe was brought to India by Jewish Iraqi traders who travelled there in the 1900s, and it now combines Indian and Arabic flavours. These little sambusaks are small pockets of dough filled with a mixture of cheddar cheese, ricotta cheese, and eggs, then baked.

CHEESE BLINTZES
Keeping to the cheese theme, cheese blintzes are another traditional dessert – but these originate from the Jews of Eastern Europe. They are warm, thin crepes rolled up with a sweet cheese filling.

SHAVUOT AROUND THE WORLD

Shavuot is a time to celebrate receiving the Torah and the moment the Jewish people became a Jewish nation. It is also a harvest festival. In most countries, Shavuot takes place in early summer, and has a focus on nature, family and delicious food. Of course, different countries and cultures have their own traditions. Let's find out about some of them!

ISRAEL
The Torah is often compared to water: as in, it is the source of life for the Jewish people. Happy with any excuse for a water fight, children in Israel often run off to have a Shavuot water fight with their friends.

SALONIKA
The Jews of Salonika, Greece (many of whom were originally from Spain and Portugal), used to bake a special Shavuot bread called *siete cielos*, which means "seven heavens". A ball of dough, representing Mount Sinai, is formed in the centre and surrounded by seven rings of dough, representing the seven heavens of God. The bread is decorated with symbolic elements, such as a Torah scroll or Jacob's ladder.

UK
The custom to eat dairy foods over Shavuot lends itself to lots of delicious dishes. Some synagogues in the UK lay out an ice cream party for children after the Shavuot prayer service. Adults can join too – if they're quick enough!

YEMEN
Sabaya is a savoury Yemenite bread, made with circular layers of thin dough, brushed with butter, sprinkled with spices, then baked. Yemenite communities in Israel still make sabaya, particularly in honour of Shavuot.

JERUSALEM
Just like the ancient Jews brought their first produce to the Temple in Jerusalem, Israeli farmers bring samples of their fruits and vegetables to the president in Jerusalem around the time of Shavuot.

NEW ZEALAND
Instead of cheesecake, New Zealanders prepare a perfect pavlova for their Shavuot feasts. The meringue-and-cream dessert was inspired by the Russian ballet dancer Anna Pavlova after she visited New Zealand in the 1920s.

LET'S MAKE CHEESECAKE!

Sweet, creamy cheesecake makes a really decadent dessert. You can add all sorts of flavours or toppings to make your cheesecake look and taste exactly how you want. This no-bake cheesecake recipe is easy, fun, and simply delicious!

Ingredients

Graham cracker crust
- 200g graham cracker crumbs
- 65g brown sugar
- 115g melted butter

Cheesecake
- 300ml heavy cream
- 680g cream cheese
- 100g sugar (granulated is best)
- 15g icing sugar
- 60g sour cream (room temperature)
- 1 tsp vanilla extract

Method

1. Mix the crust ingredients together and press the mixture tightly into a springform pan. Freeze for 15 minutes.
2. Use a mixer with the whisk attachment to whip the heavy cream until it forms stiff peaks.
3. In another bowl, use the whisk again to beat cream cheese and sugar together until smooth and creamy. Add icing sugar, sour cream, and vanilla. Beat for a few more minutes until smooth.
4. Fold the whipped cream into the cream cheese mixture until combined.
5. Spread the filling into the crust and smooth the top.
6. Cover tightly and refrigerate for at least 8 hours, or overnight.
7. Serve with toppings of your choice.

MIX IT UP!

Here are some ideas to inspire you on your cheesecake adventures!

Drizzle on a caramel sauce and other fun toppings!

Top with fresh fruit or mousse.

Spinkle cookie crumbs on top.

Are you brave enough to try different layers?

SHAVUOT CRAFT IDEAS

Make a Shavuot Card

Get out your craft materials and design some Shavuot cards for your friends and family. Use coloured paper to cut out and craft some plants and flowers. Stick them to pieces of folded card and write your Shavuot greetings inside.

Create a Flower Garland

Shavuot is all about the flowers! Create a flower garland to wear or as decoration for your home. Use carboard or string to create a base in the shape of a ring. Then pick or craft a selection of stunning flowers and use them to cover the base. Keep them in place with twine, string or tape. Wear your garland with pride!

DECORATE YOUR OWN FLOWER WALL

Can you think of creative ways to decorate your home with Shavuot flowers? What could you use as hanging baskets? Will you go for a certain colour scheme or will it simply be an explosion of colour?

DESIGN YOUR OWN MOUNT SINAI

Recreate the beautiful, flower-covered Mount Sinai – where the Jewish people received the Torah. Find a round rock and paint it with whichever colours you want. How do you imagine Mount Sinai looked on that special day all those years ago?

Tell Me More!
NEW IDEAS FOR KIDS

First published in Great Britain in 2024
by **TELL ME MORE Books**

Text copyright ©2024 Shari Last
Design copyright ©2024 Shari Last

ISBN: 978-1-917200-02-8

Picture credits: Thanks to Ronit Treatman, Adobe Stock, Leo Roza and Mateusz D at Unsplash, Cottonbro and Polesie Toys at Pexels, and Adike, Antonina Vlasova, Hadasit, James Steidl, Tomertu, and Zaid Javed at Shutterstock.

All rights reserved. Without limiting the rights under the copyright reserved above, no part of this publication may be reproduced, stored in, or introduced into a retrieval system, or transmitted, in any form, or by any means (electronic, mechanical, photocopying, recording or otherwise), without the prior written permission of the copyright owner.

WWW.TELLMEMOREBOOKS.COM

THINGS I'VE LEARNED...

Visit our website if you want to learn more about all sorts of interesting things!

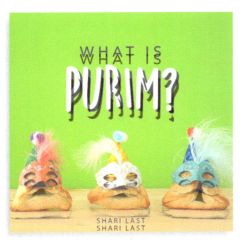 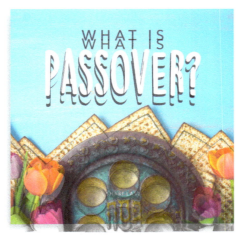 

What is Purim?   What is Passover?   What is Hanukkah?

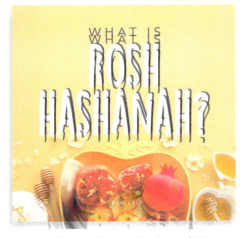 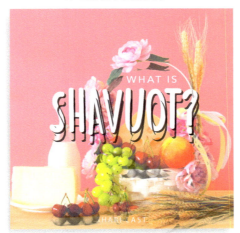 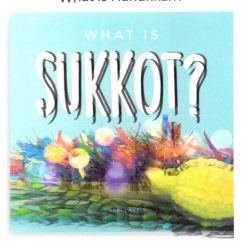

What is Rosh Hashanah?   What is Shavuot?   What is Sukkot?

COLLECT THEM ALL!

WWW.TELLMEMOREBOOKS.COM